SYMBOLS OF AMERICA

THE US FLAG

BY WALTER LAPLANTE

Gareth Stevens
PUBLISHING

Please visit our website, www.garethstevens.com. For a free color catalog of all our high-quality books, call toll free 1-800-542-2595 or fax 1-877-542-2596.

Library of Congress Cataloging-in-Publication Data

LaPlante, Walter.
The US flag / Walter LaPlante.
pages cm. — (Symbols of America)
Includes index.
ISBN 978-1-4824-1882-8 (pbk.)
ISBN 978-1-4824-1881-1 (6 pack)
ISBN 978-1-4824-1883-5 (library binding)
1. Flags—United States—Juvenile literature. I. Title.
CR113.L34 2015
929.9'20973—dc23

2014026085

Published in 2015 by
Gareth Stevens Publishing
111 East 14th Street, Suite 349
New York, NY 10003

Designer: Sarah Liddell and Laura Bowen
Editor: Kristen Rajczak

Photo credits: Cover, p. 1 VisionsofAmerica/Joe Sohm/Photodisc/Getty Images; p. 5 gary718/Shutterstock.com; p. 7 Kean Collection/Staff/Archive Photos/Getty Images; p. 9 Jorge Salcedo/Shutterstock.com; p. 11 (main) DEA PICTURE LIBRARY/De Agnosti Picture Library/Getty Images; p. 11 (inset) DevinCook/Wikimedia Commons; p. 13 Carl Lindberg/Wikimedia Commons; pp. 15 (13 stars in rows, 13 stars in circle, 30 stars), 17 jacobulus/Wikimedia Commons; p. 15 (20 stars, 38 stars) Gunter Kuchler/Wikimedia Commons; p. 19 Ariel Skelley/Blend Images/Getty Images; p. 21 Elyse Lewin/Photographer's Choice/Getty Images.

Printed in the United States of America

CPSIA compliance information: Batch #CW15GS: For further information contact Gareth Stevens, New York, New York at 1-800-542-2595.

CONTENTS

Boldface words appear in the glossary.

Flying Free

One of the most honored **symbols** of the United States is something you probably see every day—the US flag! The red, white, and blue found on the flag remind us of our nation's history and freedom.

First Flags

At the start of the American Revolution, a flag called the Continental Colors was flown. On June 14, 1777, the **official** flag was agreed upon. It would have 13 stars on a blue field and 13 red and white stripes.

CONTINENTAL COLORS, 1776

It's commonly said Betsy Ross sewed the first flag. That's likely untrue. Records from the **Continental Congress** show Francis Hopkinson, a congressman from New Jersey, **designed** it. The circle design of the stars was copied from a painting.

DESIGN FROM 1777

Stars and Stripes

The flag became very important once the colonies won their freedom from England. The 13 stars and 13 stripes stood for the colonies that became the first states in the new country. What happened to the US flag as the country grew?

By 1794, two more states had been added. The US flag now had 15 stars and 15 stripes! An 1818 law fixed the number of the flag's stripes at 13. The stars would always equal the number of states.

1814

On the July 4 following the addition of a new state, a new star would be added to the flag. For many years, it was up to flag makers to decide how to do this. There were lots of star designs as a result!

Making It Uniform

The flag's **proportions** and star design were made uniform, or to look all the same, in 1912. The stars would be in rows and each star would point upward. In 1934, the exact shades of the colors on the flag were set, too.

1934

Colors

The meaning of each color dates back to the Continental Congress. White stands for **purity**. Red means bravery. Blue symbolizes fairness and truth. Today, people often display or wear these colors together to symbolize their allegiance, or loyalty, to the United States.

Long May It Wave

Do you know the Pledge of Allegiance? It honors the flag! We celebrate Flag Day on June 14 every year, too. There are laws about how to treat the flag. They help everyone show honor and respect to this important symbol!

TIMELINE OF THE US FLAG

1776
The Continental Colors is flown as the unofficial flag.

1777
The Continental Congress establishes the first official US flag.

1794
The flag has 15 stars and 15 stripes.

1818
A law sets the number of stripes at 13.

1912
The proportions of the US flag are established.

1934
The exact colors of the flag are set.

1949
President Harry S. Truman establishes June 14 as Flag Day.

GLOSSARY

Continental Congress: a meeting of colonial representatives before, during, and after the American Revolution

design: to create the pattern or shape of something. Also, the pattern or shape of something.

official: having the support of a group

proportions: the sizes of parts of an object and how they fit together and compare to each other and the whole

purity: being free from faults

symbol: a picture, shape, or item that stands for something else

FOR MORE INFORMATION

BOOKS

Ferry, Joseph. *American Flag: The Story of Old Glory.* Broomall, PA: Mason Crest, 2014.

Herrington, Lisa M. *The American Flag.* New York, NY: Children's Press, 2014.

WEBSITES

National Symbol: The Flag
www.usconsulate.org.hk/pas/kids/sym_flag.htm
Read all about the US flag as well as other national symbols, famous Americans, and places around the country.

The United States Flag
www.ducksters.com/history/united_states_flag.php
Learn more about the flag's history and find links to many other sites of historical information.

Publisher's note to educators and parents: Our editors have carefully reviewed these websites to ensure that they are suitable for students. Many websites change frequently, however, and we cannot guarantee that a site's future contents will continue to meet our high standards of quality and educational value. Be advised that students should be closely supervised whenever they access the Internet.

INDEX